IMMUNITY FROM JUSTICE
PAT'S STORY

D1039702

BETSY DALE ADAMS

Betsy Dale Adams

MASCOT®
BOOKS

Without the help and support of others, my journey of writing this story would have never been able to become a reality. I would like to fondly thank my dear husband Patrick Adams for his support and patience, and believing in my cause. My twin sister Amanda Dale Finley for her advice and support while we both relived sad and difficult memories while writing this. My dear mother Joyce, aunts Joy and Bee, and Uncle John for their support and assistance with my research. And a special gratitude to Mr. Jere Beasley must be extended for his contribution regarding the trials that followed my brother's tragic and untimely demise. Thank you to each and every one of you for helping me make this long, overdue story possible.

As a classmate of Pat Dale's and a friend of his family, I commend Pat's sister, Betsy, for honoring her brother by telling his story and revealing, yet again, that justice, though our constant goal, can be hard to attain and that public safety often takes a backseat to politics.

Sue Bell Cobb
Alabama Supreme Court Chief Justice (Ret.)

To The Reader

While pondering the world we live in, one must reflect on whether we have progressed or regressed as a safe and civilized society.

It's easy to believe that values maintain the core of our country as safe and civil. I realized many years ago that the story of my older brother, Patrick, is an important lesson to learn. No one is immune from tragedy. When pain is inflicted upon a family and community, it should not be ignored and swept under the rug. Learning from the tragedy, we can make our society a better place for future generations.

This is not a perfect nation.

But with this in mind, we each must strive to improve our society. I have carried this story inside of me for thirty years, and the time has come for others to learn about it. Terrible misfortunes do not have to be endured in vain.

There are huge gaps in laws that are supposed to keep us safe. There are many people who need help, but can't get it due to our political process. Don't turn your head and look away. Take this book as you wish, but don't forget you can make a difference.

Requests for permission to make copies of any part of the work
should be submitted online at info@mascotbooks.com or mailed to
Mascot Books, 560 Herndon Parkway #120, Herndon, VA 20170.

ISBN-13: 978-1-62086-975-8
Library of Congress Control Number: 2014921132
CPSIA Code: PRB1214A

Printed in the United States

www.mascotbooks.com

IMMUNITY FROM JUSTICE
PAT'S STORY

BETSY DALE ADAMS

Foreword

As a lawyer, there are certain cases that stay with you. The event that took the life of Patrick Dale and forever changed the lives of his family is one of those cases. Pat, only 27 years old, was killed in July 1983 when a disturbed man he didn't even know–but who he was trying to help–shot him and robbed him and stole his car. The man who would eventually be convicted of Pat's murder, Douglas Griffin, had been diagnosed with mental illness. He had been confined to a treatment facility. Inexplicably, he was released, despite having told the doctors there that he intended to hurt people. He was allowed access to a gun–the gun he later used to kill Pat without mercy or even much thought.

Following the murder trial, my law partner Greg Allen and I became involved in the case. We worked on behalf of the family to discover why Griffin was released from a mental health facility. We tried to figure out how this unbalanced man could get access to a gun. We were hindered by state immunity laws that allow for a person's guilt while at the same time making him immune from responsibility for his actions. We ran up against opponents of so-called "gun control," despite the fact that calling for responsible gun ownership is a far cry from calling to take away someone's second amendment rights. These are battles we are still fighting.

Sadly, in the three decades since, the issues of gun control and mental illness still plague America. Reports of gun violence seem to be increasing every day. In this book, Pat's sister, Betsy Dale Adams, says it better than I ever could: "A family has lost a son, a brother, a father. Some things we have learned we cannot change, but other things we can. Some things we can fight to change; and we must."

Jere L. Beasley
Principal & Founder
Beasley, Allen, Crow, Methvin, Portis & Miles, P.C.

Chapter 1
July 15, 1983

///

It was just another Friday at work. My brother Patrick was having lunch at the plant where he, my father, aunt, and uncle worked. Aunt Pearl made a pot of her delicious beef stew and was sharing with Pat and Uncle John. Pat could eat his weight in food, and she loved sharing her recipes with family when she could. It was a hot day, so they ate in the break room where it was air conditioned. Enjoying the small talk, and Pat with his occasional knee slap of a joke, they enjoyed each other's company. Discussing the possible events of the upcoming weekend, all was well, and soon they were ready to get back to the tasks at hand at this close-knit family business. Pat thanked Pearl for her wonderful meal, and returned to the plant to finish out the workday.

Later in the day, around six o'clock, big brother Pat was at my parents' house, where we grew up, in the small, southern town of Evergreen, Alabama. They were enjoying a nice summer evening grilling hamburgers out on the deck. It was payday and Friday night - time to relax and forget about life for a while. When we cook out, we usually eat at the picnic table which is right next to the grill. All this is on the beautiful deck my father built under a great magnolia tree. Daddy is in charge of the grill with his scotch and water, and Pat with a beer. This summer evening, it was just the three of them: our parents and Pat. The evening was cooling off from a hot, humid day. The birds were busy at the bird feeders hanging from huge oak trees that surrounded the house.

This big, three-acre yard is like a sanctuary with small critters all around. Rabbits or Harvey as Dad fondly gave them all that name, squirrels, box turtles, and every kind of songbird you can imagine were all a constant source of entertainment and serenity. In the early morning, deer graze in both the front and back yards, at the edge of the woods, and alongside the turtles and other wildlife. It is a place to reflect, relax and be at peace with the world.

After enjoying their delicious meal, Pat and my stepmother Joyce were discussing the chimney sweeps that had nested in the fireplace in the den. She wanted to get the little birds out of there, as they were very noisy. Pat, being a gentle type of person who always respected nature, gathered the chicks out of the fireplace and placed them in a pie dish. He carried the little family of birds to a safe place behind the garage, next to the woods and a pecan tree. He left them there, feeling confident they would finish their growing and take to flight, as they were almost ready to fly at that point anyway. To Pat, no matter how small and insignificant one life may seem, he knew it had a right to live.

The next day, my parents were going sailing for the weekend. Depending on the weather, they would either stay in the motorhome at the dock, or sail in Escambia Bay and anchor overnight in Pensacola Bay. This was their usual weekend, or they would take the motorhome on those beloved mini-vacations to the many beautiful areas of the Gulf Coast or up to northern Alabama. They all had a very nice visit that evening. Pat bid his farewell until next time and went on his way in search of the younger crowd in the small, southern

Alabama town.

Being recently divorced, Pat was heading home to shower and change. Then he had plans to go to the lounge where friends were gathering to socialize and hear some music. He had a freshly cashed paycheck stuffed in his wallet, and was content to relax and enjoy a few laughs with old friends. The Holiday Inn Lounge in Evergreen was always a nice place to gather. There was a dance floor and usually a band. Pat was anticipating a good evening, as was he was striving to regain some kind of normalcy in his life. The divorce was so recent, so painful, that it left him financially and emotionally devastated. His ex-wife stripped him to the core. He loved her so much. She was three months pregnant and had two other young children when they met. It seemed obvious she was looking for financial security with Pat and he bit - hook, line, and sinker. When the baby was born, he took on all ownership as father. The new bride had her cake and ate it too.

Their marriage lasted about two and a half years. During that time, Pat helped his new wife get her GED High School Diploma and start college. He wanted to help her in every way, to help turn her past around and learn how to become a productive and respected member of society. As she was going forward with turning her life in a new and positive direction, we rallied around her as a family. But Pat was always her backbone of support. He wanted her to succeed and be who he thought she could and would be. This lasted about one year past the birth of her baby. Toward the end she began going out with her friends at night, dancing and staying out late, while Pat cared for the baby at home. People would tell him what they saw her doing out on the dance floor with other men, but Pat would deny it. Deep down he knew, but he still supported her. He wanted to have a wife, a child, and a home. We knew then that she only wanted financial support and someone to take care of the baby so she could resume her previous ways. The marriage started to take its toll on Pat, although he still loved her. Pat finally filed for divorce after Dad talked him into it. She had begun having an affair with another man in Evergreen, and she was draining Pat financially. She dropped out of college and reverted back to her old ways. His heart was broken, as was his dream of having a family. He moved into an apartment in town, and adopted a cat for his new companion.

As time progressed, Pat was trying to regain his independence and life back. He started dating again and was seeing Robin, a friend of mine in Fort Walton Beach, Florida, where I lived. This was not a serious or fulltime relationship, but I thought it was a start. Pat was also casually dating another friend in Evergreen, Rhonda, a girl he had known and was close friends with for years. He had lost weight and was down to about 140 pounds at 5-foot-10, and was in deep debt. His now ex-wife had taken his only credit card with her when she left him for another man. He was also in a severe depression, but was starting to climb out of the trenches again, and I was determined to help him.

Pat was Dad's right-hand man in the company at age twenty-seven. They would work ten or eleven hour days, and Pat had a bright future with the company. They re-manufactured trucks for various industries such as delivery trucks and buses. It was a financially unstable time for the country, and all industries were looking at ways to cut expenses, all the way to the corporate level. The business was profitable and growing. Daddy was grooming Pat to one day take over the business. That was certainly Dad's as well as Pat's long-term goal. It was the early 80s, and almost everyone was trying to reinvent new ways to stretch a dollar. Truck re-manufacturing seemed to be the way to go.

My father was a brilliant mechanical engineer, had designed and built trucks and buses, and was a pioneer in the recreational vehicle industry. Being one of the original designers of Airstream trailers, he went on to start early motor homes back in the 60s. Eventually he started his own line of motor homes, the Mobilux which was the crown jewel of his career. At least one was always proudly displayed in our driveway, except of course on weekends or holidays when we would be out on some expedition or on the sailboat we owned.

Daddy was an adventurous person, a virtue that he passed along to his children. No grass ever grew under our feet in our childhood years. My father taught us that if you have a vision, pursue it; the reward will be there, however you perceive it to be. If you persevere, you will succeed. He also was a lover of nature, teaching us all things that mother earth shows us possess beauty. If we had storms while on the sailboat, we would endure and eventually get through it, even if they would last two or three days. I finally came to the conclusion that these events would only make me a stronger person, and would add to my character. I still carry this lesson with me. What an admirable, humble, gentle, but strong man our father was.

Pat arrived at the lounge. He was greeted by his usual Friday night crowd. They started enjoying a few beers and were unwinding from the long work week. At another table, there was what appeared to be a rather intoxicated man that Pat and his friends did not recognize. He was loud and belligerent, asking people to buy him drinks. It seemed he was harassing one of the waitresses. They all tried to ignore him and go on with their evening, all agreeing that every town has its rednecks and troublemakers.

Pat and his friends were getting restless. The weather was nice and tomorrow was Saturday. What about a road trip to a waterpark or the beach in Mobile? Maybe they could get a few hours' sleep and be there when the park opened in the morning. With eager anticipation, a game plan was agreed upon by all.

Prior to ending the night, Pat got out to the parking lot and advised his friends he'd be giving the overly-drunk newcomer a ride home. Ever the Good Samaritan, he told his friends he would be right back. As Pat was getting into his car, a sheriff's deputy was turning around in the parking lot of the lounge. He stopped and asked Pat why he had this man in his car, and Pat said, "To give him a ride home."

The deputy just looked at him with slight suspicion as he knew Pat did not know this man. It was getting late by this time; the lounge would be closing soon. Pat's friends would stay for another round of music. They figured by that time he would return and they would say goodnight until tomorrow. They waited and waited, but Pat never returned. Finally, assuming he was tired and went home, the group took off, planning to meet in the morning.

Chapter 2
July 18, 1983

---///---

After a weekend of sailing, my parents spent Sunday night in the motorhome at the dock. They got up early Monday morning and drove back to Evergreen, arriving at the house around nine o'clock. The phone rang, and it was Aunt Pearl. She was asking if they knew where Pat was, as he never called or showed up for work. Not thinking much of it at the time, Daddy went into the office assuming Pat would come in later, remembering that Pat had a new girlfriend in Fort Walton Beach. The day progressed uneventfully, but Pat never showed up for work, nor did he call.

Monday evening after getting home from work, I received a call from my father asking me if I had seen Pat, or if I knew if he was out traveling. Pat had thought about coming down that Saturday to see me in Fort Walton Beach, but had decided not to. I had no idea what he was up to that weekend. He was here the weekend before, however. The two of us went to Navarre Beach and watched a fisherman bring a 250-pound Tarpon fish onto the Navarre Pier, the largest fish ever caught on that pier. The Navarre Pier is one of the longest piers in the Gulf of Mexico. He and I had experienced a renewed closeness since his divorce. I was a support system for him in his transition. I called my friend Robin, whom he had been dating, but she had not seen or heard from him. I shrugged it off as "Pat is twenty-seven years old, a big boy, and can take care of himself."

The next day, my dad called back. Pat was nowhere to be found. His apartment was untouched, the cat was hungry, and his car was gone. My father was beside himself. He couldn't eat or sleep. My parents drove down to Florida in the hope of any leads, and even drove to see Robin, just grasping at anything. My Aunt Joy, who was Chief Clerk of Courts, worked for a judge in Wilcox County, about fifty miles north of Evergreen. She had close ties with law enforcement, worked with Sheriff Moody Maness of Wilcox County, and was ready to follow any leads or other options. Later that day Dad contacted her, so Joy immediately put the wheels in full motion. Sheriff Maness immediately contacted the NCIC (National Crime Information Center), and put out an APB (all-points-bulletin) over the Southeastern U.S., along with a description of Pat's car.

Words cannot describe the feeling of having a loved one, an immediate family member, just disappear without a trace. It eats at you like a cancer. It has to be one of the most helpless feelings in the world.

My twin sister Amanda was living in Tuscaloosa at the time. She worked as a nurse at a hospital in Northport, the north end of the city. My oldest brother, Brad, lived in Pensacola and worked as a piano instructor and organist. We all were sick with worry. By this time, everyone in the town of Evergreen knew something was terribly wrong, but no one mentioned the unspeakable. It was too overwhelming to cross that line. We held out hope that he would just come driving up to the house, out on some crazy joy ride or having just run into an old friend and decided to go on a road trip spur of the moment. Even though that would be out of character for Pat, we hoped that was what he did. One just has an irrational kind of hope in their soul, as hope is all you have to hold on to.

The APB was out, so all we could do was let the authorities do their jobs. The local sheriff of Evergreen, Edwin Booker, was also working around the clock, interviewing people that saw him last, trying to put the pieces of the puzzle together to find my brother.

July 20, 1983

On Wednesday, my out-of-town relatives headed to the nearby town of Selma with some of their friends to buy material to make bridesmaid dresses for a cousin's upcoming wedding. As they made their way down those country roads from one town to another, they drove by a pull-over picnic area. They smelled a skunk. "Whew!" one person said. "Let's keep going. Someone needs to take a bath in here!" They laughed, all proclaiming they had had their "monthly bath". All were eager and excited about my cousin's upcoming wedding, and the beautiful dresses they were having made. Later that day, Aunt Joy received a phone call from one of her co-workers in Camden at the courthouse where she worked. A body had been discovered outside of town in the countryside. She and my uncle went to the scene, but it was "hot," full of investigators and roped off. They were not allowed to approach the body, however, they were told that there was a belt on the body, and the buckle said "Pat". The investigators thought it may be their nephew. At that time, no positive identification could be made, but they were almost certain it was Patrick Dale. A dry cleaner receipt with Pat Dale's name was found on the ground close to the body. Joy and Uncle Percy were told that they should go to my parents' house then, as Sheriff Booker of Evergreen was being notified and would be going there very soon. State Investigator Chuck Gibson was heading up the crime scene, and the Mobil Crime

Scene Unit had arrived. Joy and Percy headed south toward Evergreen. As the afternoon grew late and evening was setting in, my cousins and their friends were returning from their shopping trip in Selma. They drove back by the location where they had smelled the skunk, but now saw a blocked-off area with yellow tape. They realized it may not have been a skunk they smelled at all, but maybe something worse than a dead animal. Still not aware that a body had been discovered a few hours before, they knew that there must have been some kind of crime committed, but certainly were not aware that it was their cousin and friend, Pat. Upon arriving at my parents' home, Sheriff Booker knocked on the door. My folks knew what was happening. Daddy went into shock.

After working all day, I was weary and exhausted from worry about my brother. At home that evening, my husband and I were trying to have a normal Wednesday night, cooking supper and watching M.A.S.H., our favorite nightly show, for a little comedy relief. It was about 7:30 p.m. when I received the phone call from my parents. The news took me to the floor. A body had been found between Selma and Camden. No positive identification had been made, but there was a preliminary ID, and it was almost established that the body was Pat. The body had the belt with a buckle that said "Pat," which he wore all the time. I knew then, it was him. I went into shock. One forgets how to breathe, how to stand, how to think, when this type of trauma takes you over. Badly decomposed from the July heat and injuries sustained, the body was transported to a forensic lab in Mobile where positive identification was made with an old scar on the bottom of his foot. There was no DNA testing at that time. The reality of our lives came crashing down upon us. Richard tried to console me and read Bible verses to me until I passed out with exhaustion. The following days were a living nightmare, with no hope waking up from the bad dream. But what happened to my father and stepmother was beyond words.

There is something to be said about the phrase, "You are not supposed to bury your children." My world came to a screeching halt. I had been married three months, it should have been a happy time, but not anymore. Every one of us went into a state of shock. The state my father was in was indescribable. It was like living a nightmare without waking up. The next morning was the trip north to Evergreen, along with my siblings and their families making their respective treks to my parents' house where we all grew up. The trip usually took about two hours from where I lived, but that time it seemed to take forever. Everything was in slow motion. My shock was like nothing I had ever felt before. Yes, my biological mother died when I was nine, but that was somehow different. I was a little girl and she had been sick. That was a different kind of shock then. After finding out about Pat, I felt thick. That is the best way to describe it. It's like you pinch yourself but you can't feel it. You're numb, you forget how to breathe and you have no concept of time. Your significant other becomes your caregiver in almost all aspects. I was realizing on that trip north that there were so many unanswered questions.

Upon arrival at my folks' house, I quickly learned that they were in worse shape than I was. This was the father and stepmother of Pat. My father was clearly in shock, which worried me even worse. My stepmother, Joyce, had become his caregiver. My siblings lived farther away, so we were the first to arrive, except of course for my nearby aunts and uncles who were taking care of communication with law enforcement. Everything was up in the air. I had no idea what day it was from one to the next. The detectives, investigators, and sheriff departments were working as hard as they could to find out who did this to Pat. Then word came that Pat's car had been discovered abandoned at the very hospital where my sister Amanda worked in Northport, adding to the horror of what was unfolding before us. When she learned of this, she started wrestling with the notion that she should have seen the car and recognized it, somehow preventing this horrific act, even though Tuscaloosa was more than 100 miles from the crime scene. It was a natural reaction to have, one she eventually overcame. We all gathered at my parents' home in Evergreen, all of us in shock, especially my father. It was so incredibly painful to see a strong man in that condition. My stepmother's extended family came to our side and took care of us, along with the small and close-knit town of Evergreen.

Friday, July 22, 1983

Another day went by with still no arrest, but the people who last saw Pat were providing the police and investigators with valuable and solid information. What began to unfold was one lead after another, as well as plenty of evidence, especially after the car was found. It became obvious that Pat had been kidnapped, robbed and murdered, but not necessarily in that order. The story told by Pat's friends singled out a suspect: the same man that Pat had given a ride home. The bartender said the man had tried to start trouble at the bar and had harassed one of the waitresses. One of the waitresses refused to serve him any more alcohol, but he just went to another and got served. According to those questioned, he was loud, aggressive, intoxicated, and belligerent. He had lived in the Tuscaloosa area before, and had an ex-wife there. With this solid lead, the facts started falling into place quickly. Now there was a full-on manhunt for the suspect, a man named Douglas Griffin.

Meanwhile my dad, as a natural reaction, wanted to become part of the "chase" to get this monster that took his beloved son from him. He was a wreck. How could this have happened? Why did this happen? Why Pat, one of the most likable, peaceful people in the world? He was only twenty-seven, had a new life in front of him, and was just getting back on his feet from the divorce. There was no long illness with Pat, no anticipated death, no second opinions, no bargaining chips, no yield sign, and there was no time to say goodbye.

Sheriff Booker would come by several times a day and privately confer with my parents and Aunt Joy on the progress of the investigation. I was told by Joy that he would make a pact with my father each visit, asking him not to leave the house and allow them to do their work. That seemed to work, but he was in shock and wouldn't have been able to drive anyway.

Chapter 3

There will always be a time in life when you learn who your true friends are. This was one of those times. Our extended family from near and far came to us. Pat was well-known and liked by all for many years in the town that we grew up in. Things like this aren't supposed to happen in a small, sleepy town like Evergreen. There were no drugs involved, no reason or motive as far as we could tell. Pat only drank an occasional beer and never even dabbled in drugs. The people of Evergreen brought food and offered support every day. They were also shaken by this tragedy.

We had been notified that Pat's body had been returned from the crime lab in Mobile to the funeral home in Evergreen. Early on Friday afternoon, someone had to go to the funeral home. Brad, Amanda, and I were entrusted to make the arrangements. Daddy was in no condition to even begin that task. The three of us got through it. I'm not sure where the strength to do certain things comes from while in such a state of shock, but we got through it. We were to gather at the funeral home later that Friday evening, and Pat's memorial was going to be the following day. The funeral director, Sam Cope, told us it was to be closed casket due to the deteriorated condition of Pat's body. All we could do was say okay, but we were not even sure what that meant. We just stared at him with humble and bewildered acceptance. The manhunt was still ongoing, but we were going forward with Pat's memorial.

In the middle of the afternoon just after we got back from the funeral home, Sheriff Booker came to the house. No arrest had been made, but they had located the suspect, Douglas Griffin. He was an inpatient at the Evergreen Hospital. We learned that he had been admitted with an apparent drug and alcohol overdose, and a possible attempted suicide. He was the prime suspect in the murder, so an arrest would be imminent. We were told he was in an unconscious state there. Booker said they wanted to complete the investigation before an arrest would be made. The administrator of the hospital, Bill McKenzie, just so happened to be our next door neighbor. He and his wife had already been to our house before he was told about the suspect. When he learned of Griffin, he returned to our house in a gesture of support. When Sheriff Booker told my father the news of the whereabouts of Griffin, my father put on his shoes and tried to head out the door. He was determined to get to him and kill him right there in the hospital. Aunt Joy got on her knees and begged him not to, and to allow the law to do its work. In his sheer state of exhaustion and shock, he succumbed to her plea. From that point on, a 24-hour watch was put in place for my father not to leave and go to the hospital, which was ten minutes from the house.

The Friday night visitation, of course, was to be closed casket. My mother's death and the pain we all endured back in 1967 echoed in my heart at that time. The "why" from a nine-year-old girl losing her mother; similar emotions arise from losing someone so close at such a young age, but the violence of this tragedy ripped through me like a double-edged sword. I could see the support there that night. The minister was there for my family; practically everyone in Evergreen that knew Pat was there. Daddy, it appeared, was going to try to open the casket, but it was secured. He had to bury his son, but he wanted to see him first. It was as if my brother was his little boy again, and he wanted to hold him and tell him he loved him dearly, just one more time. The pain I witnessed and endured that evening was unparalleled to anything in my life. His son, my brother, in a closed casket. All I could do was continually shake my head and ask, "Why?"

Suddenly, Sheriff Booker came walking into the room. As I looked up at him wondering why he was there, he looked at the minister and nodded, then they ushered us into a back room. An arrest had been made. We were told that Griffin had been arrested upon his gaining full consciousness and was shackled to his hospital bed. He was charged with the crime of capital murder. The reason they waited to make the arrest was because the capital murder charge had to stand "iron clad". The State wanted a capital murder charge, and they wanted it to be air tight. All the facts and evidence was in. This man, as far as I was concerned, would never see the light of day again. While we were still at the funeral home that night, a caravan of police cars and escorts went to the Evergreen Hospital, put Griffin in shackles, took him out of the hospital, and drove the fifty or so miles up to the jail in Selma, close to where the murder took place. We came out of the back room with a sigh of relief, only to turn around and see Pat's closed casket.

Saturday, July 23, 1983

The next day, Richard drove all of us in Daddy's Lincoln Towncar out to the country church for the memorial service. Just to add to the pain, we had to drive past the house that Pat drove Griffin to on that fateful Friday night, supposedly giving him a friendly ride home. It was a modest green house in the country where Griffin lived with his parents. Hundreds of people were at the church. Sheriff Booker escorted us into the driveway toward the front double doors of this small, charming, Southern church that we frequented from time to time. This is the church that my stepmother Joyce and her family grew up in.

The memorial service was as painful as I remembered my mother's service being almost exactly sixteen years earlier. The minister gave his speech and said, "We should not question God's work." I wanted to stand and say, "God had nothing to do with this! This was not God's work, and God does not use killers and drunks to murder innocent people." I will never believe that. God was not in control of what happened that night. There are people like Griffin all over the world, and they do not work for God.

The graveside was the worst; it was so final at that moment. There was not a dry eye in the vicinity. There was no turning back; it was time to turn and leave him. The moment of truth, as it hit me, was too much to bear. I remember not being able to stand. My father-in-law was on one side, Richard on the other, supporting me back to the car. Thankfully, Pat's ex-wife was nowhere to be seen. As we drove back toward Evergreen, I remember Joyce wailing in backseat. We all had our weak moments, and could not predict when it would happen. When it did with each of us, others would be strong. Maybe God had something to do with that. Back at the house, I collapsed, then slept.

Chapter 4

Our work was not done in many ways. First, we had to clean Pat's apartment out, another extremely painful task. His personal belongings, laundry, the smell of Pat in the home and the unwashed clothes, just as if he was still alive. The pet that was searching for his owner but now needed a new home. Everything had become stuck in time at his home. Life stopped in his home when he died. We could only take one day at a time. My parents left town in their motorhome and went to a State Park for a week or so just to get away from it all and contemplate the gravity of Pat's demise. My father was unable to work for many weeks after that. I know the deep, dark shock did not wear off for me for about three months. Christmas that year was a black one, very dark and somber; that is the only way I can describe it.

Am I supposed to go home and just resume my life like nothing happened? Are we supposed to say "too bad, so sad" and just go on with our lives? There had to be some kind of resolve; Pat should not have died in vain. Even though much had been discovered during the investigation following Pat's murder, there were many more questions than answers at that point. Much had to be learned, something had to come out of this to make sure this wouldn't happen again. Once again, the questions remained, "Why? Who is this Douglas Griffin? Why did he seek out a victim? Why did he pick Patrick to be his victim?" In the days, weeks, months, and even years that lay ahead, much would be uncovered and brought out as to why Patrick Dale died in the early morning hours of July 16, 1983.

First, what was Douglas Griffin's motive? Was he just wanting to kill someone for no apparent reason? Who was this man? The investigators knew a lot more than we did, but we were soon to find out. As the weeks followed, this man's history began to unfold. We learned he had recently been discharged from Bryce Hospital, a state run mental hospital in Tuscaloosa. He held a paraplegic farmer at gunpoint just weeks before killing Pat. He used the same sawed-off shotgun to kill Pat. Griffin had charges against him, but the farmer soon dropped the charges. Griffin had multiple previous indictments with a documented violent history. He had been let out of the mental hospital just seventy-two days prior to the murder. How did Griffin get the gun? He had no gun when Pat took him to his house. The evidence indicated Griffin went into his house to get a five-dollar bill for gas, but instead came out with a gun, which he held down by his side. Then he got in the car, pointed the gun at Pat, and made him drive north on a dark, country road, Highway 83, toward north Alabama. This was the initial kidnapping of Patrick.

We were told we were entitled to a "fair and speedy trial". At least that is what we were led to believe, but it turned out that was not the case. The actual trial took place nearly a year-and-a-half after the crime occurred, hardly an early trial. Every time a date was set, the defense would delay, stating repeatedly they weren't ready. No more details of the crime were brought out until we learned them at that trial. We did learn, however, that Griffin would enter a plea of self-defense. I thought that laughable given his violent reputation and past, and Griffin was at least four inches taller and sixty pounds heavier than Pat. I still, to this day, don't completely understand why a judge would allow so many delays for the trial; there had to be at least five. Finally, the trial was set for early December 1984, just before Christmas. This time there was no continuance.

The Murder Trial, First Week of December, 1984:

The State of Alabama vs. Douglas Griffin: Capital Murder

Honorable Judge Richard Norton Presiding

Griffin's plea: Self Defense.

The first day was jury selection. Douglas Griffin was escorted into the courtroom and seated to our right, on the other side of a short wooden rail. This was our first time seeing him. I always wondered what this monster looked like. He was big, as I had been told. Just sitting and facing ahead with an emotionless stare, he would not look at us. His parents were also in the courtroom. They were pointed out to me, and I had empathy for his mother. They were elderly, and appeared as if they, too, had all the stress anyone could endure. The majority of the questions toward prospective jurors asked their stance on capital punishment. Defense wanted jurors who did not believe in it, and the State wanted those who did believe it was appropriate in the case of a guilty verdict of Capital Murder. The jury was set in the late afternoon. It was an all-black jury.

Day two started out with the state putting the first witness on the stand. The courtroom was full of people: the press, extended family, friends and, of course, Douglas Griffin sitting in the front surrounded by law enforcement. He sat there, looking straight ahead, right in front of us. I looked at my father, wondering how he was controlling himself with that monster just feet away. He had wanted to get his hands on him for so long. I was prepared as best I could be. We were told by Ed Greene, State Attorney who headed up the State's case,

PATRICK FRANK DALE

Patrick Frank Dale, 27, of 209 Montesano Drive, Evergreen, died Saturday, July 16, in Wilcox County. Funeral services were held Saturday afternoon at 2 o'clock from Mt. Zion Methodist Church with the Rev. Thomas Smith officiating. Burial was in the church cemetery, Cope Funeral Home directing.

Survivors include his father, Emmett Dale, and stepmother, Mrs. Joyce Dale of Evergreen; one brother, Bradford Dale, Pensacola; two sisters, Mrs. Elizabeth Ann Coker, Fort Walton Beach, and Mrs. Amanda Findley, Tuscaloosa; and one nephew, Jessie Findley, Tuscaloosa.

PATRICK FRANK DALE
OCT. 1, 1955 — JULY 16, 1983
A FINE SON
A GOOD AND GENTLE MAN

A TRIBUTE TO PAT DALE

They shall know well the heavenly fellowship of men that perish and of summer morn. And whence they came and whither they shall go, The dew upon their feet shall manifest.

These words by Wallace Stevens should bear some meaning for those of us who knew and grew up with Pat Dale. First, we now understand better how important moments of friendship and fellowship can be. These are what our memories of Pat will be built from. Second, like the morning dew, he has disappeared.

For those who didn't know him, he was 27 years old, medium height but lanky, with dark brown hair, a sincere face and quiet disposition. In school he would be remembered as a bright student and a good musician. The several years he worked with his father were marked by ingenuity, persistence, and a willingness to put in the extra time, a readiness to pay the price for success. He was comfortable in solitude but enjoyed the company of friends. His wit was usually dry, often laced with irony and dark humor, but he could pull off a good thigh-slapper if the mood struck him. His life was beset from time to time with problems many of us face, but he always pulled himself through with calm determination. He trusted deeply and acted upon his belief that all people are basically good. He was totally non-violent. His greatest virtue, though, was surely his love and concern for his family.

Now that Pat is gone, we have no choice but to learn from his tragic and untimely demise. We must cherish to the fullest our friends, pay more attention to the world around us, and find in everyday life those signs of beauty, dignity and heroism that make the ones who remain remember that which is lost. We will miss Pat Dale, but must understand that regardless of grief and suffering, the world goes on, offering to us even now its constant lesson of how all things in this life arise and pass away.

Wallace Stevens, again, seems to speak directly to us, as we try to accustom ourselves to Evergreen without our friend among us...

Our walk upon our hills, a nd the quail
Whistle about us their spontaneous cries;
Sweet berries ripen in the wilderness;
And in the isolation of the Sky,
At evening, casual flocks of pigeons make
Ambiguous undulations as they sink,
Downward to darkness, on extended wings. (1915)
A Friend

™ JOURNAL-Advertiser

Human emotions go on display during murder trial

CAMDEN — The pain was etched on Joyce Dale's face each time another grisly detail about her son's murder surfaced during the trial.

Patrick Dale's body was found in a wooded area near Camden during the hottest part of the summer, and the description given to the jury brought back the agony his mother had hoped to forget.

The man who found Dale's body testified he was attracted by the odor and, as he got closer, two buzzards that had been feeding on the remains.

The discovery was mentioned several times by the prosecutors. On each occasion, Mrs. Dale's eyes moved from Douglas Griffin, the man accused of killing her son, to the defendant's parents, who sat in another section of the courtroom.

She said later she was looking for emotion, for sorrow.

"I didn't see any," Mrs. Dale said. "He just kept staring ahead, and they didn't seem to show any emotion either."

GRIFFIN'S MANNEQUIN gaze was fixed on a spot near the jury box. His parents sat silently behind him, suffering inwardly the pain and grief expressed openly by relatives of the victim.

ALVIN BENN

Human emotions often take a backseat at trials, as judges and attorneys argue the finer points of mind-boggling laws that frequently escape jurors and spectators.

"It's unfortunate that our laws are so complex that we must go through the machinations we saw exhibited in this trial to obtain justice," said Emmett Dale, who had been grooming his son to take over his truck-refurbishing business in Evergreen.

At one time, a jury's guilty verdict in a capital murder case was followed by a sentence and, in the case of a death decree, an execution date.

All that has changed. A capital murder conviction today is followed by a hearing — another trial, in effect — to determine life or death, a pre-sentence report and, finally, imposition of the penalty, if the judge agrees with the jury.

THE TRIAL, and sentencing hearing this week added to the agony of the Dale family. In order to present a convincing argument and obtain a conviction, the district attorney's office had to paint the most horrifying picture it could.

"It was more than a killing," assistant District Attorney Jim Sullivan told the jury. "It was an execution. He blew his head off. He blew his chest off. And then he goes to Tuscaloosa, where the parties."

If the jurors were looking for signs of remorse from Griffin, they didn't find it in the courtroom.

His lawyer said it was because Griffin was in shock.

The victim's angry relatives contended it was because he's a cold-blooded killer.

During a conference with the judge and attorneys, Griffin said he had dropped out of school after the 9th grade.

THE ONLY GRADE he ever received above a "D," he said, was the "A" he got in physical education because his height helped him make the basketball team.

At 6 feet 3 inches and 220 pounds, Griffin outweighed the victim by almost 100 pounds, and Dale's relatives said they would never buy the accused's contention that he had to fire the

![Dale]

Dale

![Griffin]

Griffin

12-gauge shotgun because Dale was rushing at him.

"He probably could have killed Patrick with his bare hands," one relative said. "He never gave him a chance. He just executed him in that field that night."

The victim's twin sisters were devastated by the murder, and developments at the trial had them in tears several times.

Elizabeth Coker and Amanda Finley loved their brother, and the hate they held for Griffin was evident from the first day.

During one break, Mrs. Coker walked toward the rail separating the court and audience sections.

TEARS STREAMING down her cheeks, she stared toward Griffin. His gaze on the edge of the jury box did not move.

"He wouldn't look at me," she said. "I never knew real hate until this happened, but I have it in my heart for him. I can never forgive him."

Her opinion was shared by other members of the family, and while no overt threats were made, security was beefed up in the courtroom because of the emotionalism evident throughout the trial.

During his closing arguments, Deputy District Attorney Ed Greene mentioned the upcoming holiday void left in the Dale family.

"There will be no presents this year, but there will be a big, empty chair," said Greene.

The jurors did not miss the emotion. They saw the tears and heard the sobs.

———
The writer covers west Alabama for The Advertiser.

THE WILCOX

Progressive

Era

CAMDEN, ALABAMA 36726 [USPS 683-920]   WEDNESDAY, DECEMBER 5, 1984

Jury to decide fate

of

accused shotgun

killer

The trial of a young Evergreen man charged with killing a fellow Evergreen resident whose body was found in a thicket just off Wilcox County Road 89 in July of last year goes into its third day this morning at the Wilcox County courthouse. Douglas Griffin, 27, is charged with murdering 29 year-old Pat Dale during the commission of a robbery and the state is asking for the death penalty.

Prosecutors from the District Attorney's office charge that the events leading up to Dale's death began when the pair happened to meet in the lounge of the Holiday Inn at Evergreen. Witnesses were produced Monday to testify that both men were at the lounge on the night before the killing took place and that they left together in the victim's car shortly before the lounge closed for the night.

Griffin's account of what happened the night of the killing is just the opposite of what the state says it will prove. He has admitted that he and Dale left the lounge together and he has not denied firing the fatal shots. He says, however, that both he and Dale had been drinking and taking drugs and that they stopped at the old roadside park to go to the bathroom. He says Dale went to the trunk of the car and got out the shotgun which he pointed at Griffin and said he was going to rob him and leave him there.

Griffin says that after an exchange of words the two wrestled over the gun and that he managed to jerk it away and fire the fatal shots. Griffin has a provable record of drug abuse and drinking but state witnesses who have already testified stated that Dale was not drunk when he left the lounge in Evergreen and that they did not know of him using drugs.

Friends of the victim told the jury that the victim, Pat Dale, and the defendant, Douglas Griffin, were not friends and that they had not come to the lounge together. One witness said he and Dale, and several other men, had gone to the restroom and that Douglas Griffin approached Pat Dale there and asked him for a ride home. The witness, lounge- waiter Robert Pugh, said Griffin agreed to pay Dale "five dollars for gas," if he would give him a ride home.

LATE DEVELOPMENTS

The trial of Douglas Griffin took a surprise turn late yesterday afternoon when the defense rested its case without calling the nearly thirty witnesses who had been expected to testify.

Judge Norton ruled that an insanity plea would not be admissible since no evidence had presented along that line.

The defendant can be found guilty, or innocent, of capital murder; guilty or innocent of murder in the first degree. It does not appear that lesser charges will be given to the jury.

The case is expected to be given to the jury for deliberation as early as 10:00 this morning.

In the event that the jury finds Griffin guilty of capital murder the same jury will then be called upon for a second "trial" to determine the penalty.

Another witness, Lydia Johnson, testified that she was working as a waitress in the lounge and that Griffin had seated himself at a place on the bar next to where the waitresses pick up their orders. She said Douglas kept bothering her and asking her to go out with him. She said she told him she could not because she had "a man at home."

She said Griffin told her that she and he could get "rid of the old man." Accounts in yesterday's Montgomery "Advertiser" incorrectly stated that Lydia Johnson, "said she was drinking at the Holiday Inn lounge...", and that, "she had a male friend at home." The Johnson woman, a state witness, did not say she was drinking and made it clear that she was an employee at the lounge. Her marital status was never mentioned.

A Conecuh County deputy, Jimmy Lambert, testified and said he was making a routine stop in the Holiday Inn parking lot when he ran into Dale and Griffin leaving together. He said he knew both of them and was a friend of Pat Dale. He said he was surprised to see them together and asked Dale what he was doing with Griffin and was told by Dale that he was giving Griffin a ride home. He said he saw them leave together in Dale's car.

Other witnesses testified that Dale had been planning on going to the beach with them the next morning and that when he did not show up they went by his residence and left a note telling him they were going ahead and for him to follow.

The state expects to prove that Griffin forced Dale to drive to Wilcox County where he killed him for the purpose of robbing him and taking his car. The prosecution claims Douglas Griffin made Dale get out of the car near an abandoned roadside park just off County Road 89 near Snow Hill and about 15 miles East of Camden. The prosecution says Griffin then shot Dale twice with a shotgun, robbed him, and then dragged the body into a thicket before taking the car to Tuscaloosa where he sold it for $200.

The state says it will also show the jury that Griffin then went to his mother's home in Evergreen where he took two bottles of pills and drank a pint of whiskey. He was then taken by family members to the hospital in Evergreen and was there when he was arrested and charged with the murder of Pat Dale.

Much of yesterday morning's trial was concerned with the admisibility of a confession which Griffin made while jailed in Selma. Investigator Chuck Gibson told the court, in the absence of the jury, that he and Sheriff Prince Arnold interviewed Griffin at the jail in Selma and took down the confession. He said Griffin was fully advised of his rights and produced a signed waiver to that effect.

Griffin then took the stand, also in the absence of the jury, and admitted signing the confession. He said, however, that during the questioning, and after signing the waiver-of-rights, he asked Gibson and Arnold to get him a lawyer but they would not. He told Circuit Judge J.C. Norton that Sheriff Arnold pounded on the table and insisted that he go ahead and, "tell the truth". He said Sheriff Arnold said he already had enough on him to "fry you in the electric chair tonight."

Griffin said he did go ahead and sign the statement but that he had wanted a lawyer. He added that sometime later he "scratched" his wrist with a razor blade and was taken to the doctor. He said when he was returned to the cell that a "new razor blade" had been left in his cell. He implied that it had been left there by jailers who had repeatedly cursed him and refused to give him the prescription drugs he was supposed to be taking. He said he did not receive his medicine until he was brought later to the jail in Camden.

Pat Dale's apparent murder is one of the most gruesome killings in Wilcox County in recent years. It was discovered on a hot, July afternoon in 1983 when Highway Department worker Emanuel Hardly discovered the body while working with a road crew. Hardly took the stand and testified that he had gone about 90 feet off the road into the thicket to use the bathroom and saw two buzzards fly out. He said he went closer and saw the body lying on the ground badly decomposed. He said the first thing he noticed was the man's shoes and the pants he was wearing. He said he did not get closer than about five feet and saw where the buzzards and other animals had apparently scratched away leaves and limbs which he thought might have been placed on the body. Hardly said he immediately radioed Mr. Eugene Phillips, the Supervisor of the Department's office in Camden. Hardly testified that he did not touch anything at the scene.

Though not yet brought out in the trial, Mr. Phillips then contacted former Wilcox County Cornoner Mark Curl to advise him that the body had been found. The Coroner at that time, the late Roman Pettway, could not be immediately located and Curl went to the scene. He was followed shortly by Camden Assistant Police Chief Robert Rogers and about an hour later by Investigator Chuck Gibson. Rogers took the stand Monday and said he went and helped secure the crime scene because no officers from the Sheriff's Department were available at that time.

After examination at the scene the body was removed to the University of South Alabama Medical Center in Mobile where a state medical pathologist determined the exact cause of death. The physician took the stand here Monday and said Dale died of shotgun wounds to the head and chest. He did not speculate which shot was fired first but indicated that either could have been fatal.

Sources outside the trial, but close to both the defense and prosecution, have said Griffin was willing Monday to plead guilty in exchange for a life sentence but this was not accepted.

Victim's Kin Block Plea Bargain

By ALVIN BENN
Advertiser Staff Writer

CAMDEN — A Wilcox County jury decides the fate Wednesday of an Evergreen man whose offer to plead guilty to murder in exchange for life in prison was rejected by the prosecution.

Conviction on the capital murder charge could lead to a death sentence or life without parole for 27-year-old Douglas Griffin.

Griffin had entered a plea of not guilty by reason of insanity in the shotgun slaying last year of Patrick Dale.

Andy Cromer, one of two court-appointed defense attorneys, said Tuesday the offer of a guilty plea in exchange for the life sentence, which would include the possibility of parole, was made last week to Deputy District Attorney Ed Greene.

"Ed relayed the proposal to the Dale family and told us they would have none of that," said Cromer. "He said they were upset and would settle for nothing short of a capital sentence."

Dale's parents, other relatives and friends listened to testimony Tuesday and chatted with Greene and his assistant, Jim Sullivan, during breaks in the trial.

Insanity Plea Ruled Out

Cromer also said Circuit Judge J. C. Norton refused to allow the insanity plea to be considered by the jury "because he did not feel there was sufficient evidence to warrant it."

Norton met with both sides in his chamber toward the close of Tuesday's session and ruled out the insanity plea consideration.

Cromer also said the jury will be allowed to consider sentences including murder and manslaughter in addition to capital murder.

Dale, 29 at the time of his death, was fatally shot on July 16, 1983, in the Snow Hill Community near Camden.

A state criminalist linked the 12-gauge shotgun and shells to Dale's decomposed body. Dale had offered to drive Griffin home from an Evergreen lounge, according to witnesses who testified earlier in the trial.

Norton did not allow graphic photographs of the body to be viewed by the all-black jury following objections by the defense that they might inflame members of the panel.

Both Griffin and Dale are white. Griffin took the stand briefly Tues-

Jury To Decide
In Shooting Trial

continued from page 1D

day and testified that he voluntarily gave a four-page statement that described events surrounding the fatal shooting.

State Trooper Investigator Chuck Gibson read the statement signed by Griffin who claimed Dale had threatened to abandon him along the road after the two had driven in Dale's car from Conecuh to Wilcox County.

Griffin claimed the two began to scuffle over the weapon he said he had picked up at his house before the two left the county. Griffin said the shotgun belonged to his father.

Dale was struck by two loads of buckshot, said Greene, who added that one nearly decapitated Dale. Greene said the second shot left a gaping chest wound.

Sold Dale's Car

Iris Dollar, a Tuscaloosa woman, testified that Griffin spent two nights with her and, during that time, he sold the 1975 Chrysler that had belonged to Dale.

Reuben Cunningham testified that he bought the car for $200, but later became suspicious and had the license tag checked out by his brother, who is a bail bondsman.

He said when he found out the car had been involved in a possible homicide, he took it to a parking lot near the Northport Police Department and later notified authorities where they could find it.

A Griffin relative, Cliff Madison, testified that the defendant gave him the shotgun to keep and asked him to remain quiet about where he got it.

Griffin's mother testified that her son has had a drinking problem for years and tried to commit suicide the day before he was arrested at the Evergreen Hospital.

Trilla Griffin said he consumed a month's worth of prescribed medicine and had to have his stomach pumped.

Jury Says Man Guilty In Killing

By ALVIN BENN
Advertiser Staff Writer

CAMDEN — A Wilcox County jury deliberated only 28 minutes Wednesday before convicting an Evergreen man of capital murder in a shotgun slaying that prosecutors called an execution.

The panel will decide Thursday whether Douglas Griffin should die in the electric chair or spend the rest of his life in prison.

"Nothing will bring back my son," said Emmett Dale, father of the victim. "I believe in the death penalty and this man deserves it. He killed once and he would kill again."

Griffin, 29, was charged with capital murder in the July 16, 1983, death of Patrick Dale, 27, whose badly decomposed, nearly decapitated body was found in a wooded area a few miles east of Camden.

The sentencing portion of the trial would have been held Wednesday afternoon, but was delayed when the father of one of the defense attorneys died at a Selma hospital.

The remaining attorney, Donny McLeod, asked Circuit Judge J.C. Norton for time to confer with his co-counsel, Andy Cromer, and the judge gave them until Thursday morning.

Deputy District Attorney Ed Greene said he will ask for the death penalty.

During closing arguments Wednesday, Greene called Griffin a "cold-blooded killer" who deserved little consideration from a jury.

"He decided it was time for Patrick Dale to die," said Greene, "and he carried it out in the most horrible and gruesome way.

"He gave Patrick Dale half a second in front of a double-ought shotgun," Greene added. "He should expect no more from you than what he gave Patrick Dale."

Struggle over Shotgun

The defense argued that Griffin and Dale had struggled over the shotgun and that the shooting was not intentional.

Cromer told the jurors they should block the road "that leads to Atmore and the electric chair."

Capital murder charges were lodged against Griffin because the victim's car was stolen. Murder committed in the course of a robbery carries either a death sentence or life without parole.

Assistant District Attorney Jim Sullivan told the jury Dale had been marched into a field where he was shot and then dragged into the woods.

"It was more than a killing," said Sullivan. "It was an execution. He blew his head off. He blew his chest off. Then he goes to Tuscaloosa where he parties."

Dale's body was discovered by a Wilcox County man who detected a strong odor, and Greene said the presence of buzzards "and other varmints" helped locate the remains.

Greene said Dale's pockets had been turned inside out, indicated the money he had carried was taken after the shooting.

Witnesses testified Dale agreed to take Griffin home from an Evergreen lounge on the night of July 15.

Griffin Given Life in Prison Without Parole

By ALVIN BENN
Advertiser Staff Writer

CAMDEN — Douglas Griffin, convicted in the shotgun slaying of an Evergreen man this past year, was sentenced to spend the rest of his life in prison Thursday.

The verdict was greeted with relief by Griffin's family and anger by the relatives of Patrick Dale, whose decomposed body was found near Camden in July, 1983.

Griffin "doesn't have a right to live," said one of Dale's sister, Amanda Finley. "He should be punished by death."

Security for the hearing was tight. A dozen state troopers and sheriff's deputies took positions throughout the room.

The all-black jury deliberated 33 minutes before voting 10-2 for life without parole instead of the death penalty. The forewoman said the decision was properly made.

Wednesday the jury spent 28 minutes deliberating before convicting Griffin, 27, of capital murder.

"The state had substantial evidence to convict him, but we also felt one wrong should not be followed by another wrong," said Minnie Pettway, a Wilcox County teacher.

Mrs. Pettway said the voting was done by secret ballot.

Mental Institutions Face Lawsuit

By RICK HARMON
Advertiser Staff Writer

The relative of a man who was shot to death by a mental patient in 1983 is suing mental health institutions, a Eufaula motel and a drug manufacturer for a total of $25 million and charging that they were partially responsible for the man's death.

The suit contends that Douglas Edward Griffin, a former mental patient who was convicted of shooting Patrick Dale to death, was known to be a "violent and dangerous person" when he was released by mental health authorities.

The suit charges that the Alabama Department of Mental Health, Bryce Hospital and the Northwest Albama Health Center were negligent in releasing Griffin.

Emmett O. Dale, the administrator of Patrick Dale's estate, is also suing a Eufaula motel, which he said served alcohol to Griffin, and a pharmaceutical company, which manufactured a drug that the suit charges caused Griffin's mental condition to become worse.

Dale was shot twice with a shotgun July 16, 1983, in an Evergreen lounge. Griffin was convicted of the shooting later that year and was sentenced in Wilcox County to life without parole.

The pharmaceutical manufacturer being sued is CIBA, a New Jersey company that made a drug that Griffin was taking for treatment of his condition.

Attorney Jere Beasley is charging that instead of improving Griffin's mental condition, the drug further impaired his mental abilities and increased his reaction to alcohol.

"Griffin had a history of unsuccesful attempts to commit suicide, was a known drug addict and was a known abuser of alcoholic beverages and prescription drugs," says the suit.

A lawyer for the Department of Mental Health would not comment on the suit.

A tale of 2 sons — 1 dead, 1 behind bars

It's like a nightmare that won't go away for the families of Patrick Dale and Douglas Griffin.

One son can only be visited at a cemetery, the other behind bars at a state penitentiary.

Mr. Griffin murdered Pat Dale five years ago — tore him apart with a shotgun blast and then left him in the woods of Wilcox County.

The trial was another reminder for the two families — one seeking vengeance and the other mercy.

Mr. Griffin was convicted of capital murder, but his life was spared, and he is to spend the rest of his days in prison.

A couple of years after the jurors returned their verdict in Wilcox County, a civil court jury in Montgomery County ordered Mr. Griffin and three employees of the state Department of Mental Health and Mental Retardation to pay $11.6 million to the Dale family.

The state appealed, claiming immunity from such things, and prevailed when the Alabama Supreme Court found in its favor.

Attorneys for the Dale family view the high court's ruling as a major mistake, a decision that could have far-reaching ramifications.

"I think the state should take away immunity from those who deal with someone known to be mentally incompetent or dangerous," says former Lt. Gov. Jere Beasley, who represented the Dale family.

Psychiatry is not an exact science such as chemistry, and the state apparently believes those who care for the mentally ill are prone to make mistakes from time to time.

Mind-reading may be a perplexing profession, but Mr. Beasley and his law partner, Greg Allen, feel there were more than enough indicators to keep Mr. Griffin in Bryce Hospital five years ago.

When a boxer rears back to throw a right hand to his opponent's head, it's known as telegraphing a punch.

The Dale family lawyers feel the same principle could be applied to Mr. Griffin, because of his prior proclivity toward violence.

He was an alcoholic as well as one of life's losers, according to court records that showed at one time "he was consuming two pints of whiskey or one case of beer per day."

He had been under psychiatric care for years before being admitted for treatment at Bryce and, along the way, was arrested several times — once when he pointed a shotgun at his employer and threatened to kill him.

bled young man who needed a lot of help.

During his treatment at Bryce, Mr. Griffin did not complete his drug and alcohol abuse program, but acknowledged writing a letter in which he threatened to kill himself and others.

Mr. Allen noted that Mr. Griffin was released from Bryce — according to one of the three mental health employees sued by the Dale family — "because he was wasting space and not cooperating with the program."

Mr. Griffin met Pat Dale at an Evergreen lounge, asked him for a ride and then kidnapped him. He forced him to drive north to Wilcox County, where he shot him in the back.

"He gave Patrick Dale half a second in front of a double-aught shotgun," said Deputy District Attorney Ed Greene, who told the jury the victim had been executed. "He decided it was time for him to die, and he carried it out in the most horrible and gruesome way."

It happened on a scorchingly hot July day and when the body was found, Mr. Greene said the presence of "buzzards and other varmints helped locate the remains."

Emmett Dale ran a successful Evergreen business, but his son's murder took everything out of him. He sold the business — intended for Pat to take over — and he and his wife moved to Florida.

If Mr. Griffin seemed remorseful, he didn't show it after the verdict when he tried to kick a photographer and struck a Conecuh County deputy by mistake.

Mr. Greene once said Mr. Griffin was "mean as a rattlesnake," and the victim's parents still are trying to reconcile his three meals a day with their son's grave.

Their lawyers believe the best way to avoid another Douglas Griffin is to make sure the patients stay at Bryce.

"This case is clear as a bell," says Mr. Beasley. "That boy should never have been let out. The law needs to be changed."

By that, he and Mr. Allen feel the blanket of immunity that covers state mental health workers should be removed in cases such as Pat Dale's death.

He pointed to the Raymond Eugene Brown case in which a man who murdered three family members years ago was paroled, only to kill two other innocent people not that long afterward.

The state Board of Pardons and Parole has "absolute immunity" over its decisions, as controversial as they may be, but Mr. Allen thinks the mental health department should not be allowed even the "qualified" immunity it now has.

He also says the department's offer of $100,000 to the Dale family a few months ago "is an admission of liability."

The offer was contingent upon the Supreme Court's not overruling the Montgomery County jury's decision — which it did this summer.

If the Legislature changes the immunity protection law for the mental health department — as Mr. Beasley suggests — it would mean the public still would suffer since any payment would come from the public treasury.

But, he argues, it would put the taxpayers' servants on notice that they should walk that extra mile to see the public is protected from the likes of Doug Griffin.

As far as Emmett Dale is concerned, he'd like to see Mr. Griffin walk one last mile, and he'd be there to do more than just watch.

"I'd be happy to pull the switch," he said, after the jury spared the life of the man who had murdered his son.

The writer covers West Alabama for The Advertiser.

Sunday, Sept 18, 1988

that we would hear graphic details of the crime in order to "move" the jury. The first witness was a county road worker who had stopped at the roadside picnic area to relieve himself. He testified that he smelled a foul odor but thought nothing of it, assuming it was a dead animal in the brush. He got back into his truck and left. The very next day, he made the same stop for the same reason. He did mention that he had never stopped there before, and certainly not two days in a row. I thought that this may have been some divine coincidence, or at least I chose to believe this because of the need to find Pat. His testimony was shocking and sickening. He said he got out of his truck, went to the same spot in the woods, but this time the foul odor was unbearable. Upon looking in the direction of the smell, he saw something that would change his life forever. His face then contorted into sad disgust when he explained what happened next. He saw several large buzzards well into the brush, and then he focused on a pair of blue jeans right in the middle of the large birds. He took steps toward it; the buzzards all flapped their large wings and flew away. We became very distraught at this time, but maintained our composure. Then Attorney Greene asked him if he saw the face of a person, or a head, and the witness said, "There was no face or head sir." All he saw were jeans, shoes, and badly decomposed and only partial remains, but no head. The people in the courtroom let out a sickening sigh and mutter of disgust that echoed an overwhelming feeling of sadness and hurt for Patrick. That is all the first witness needed to say to start the trial. He stepped down. The difficulty with this was they were talking about my brother Patrick, a person, a good person. To this day I cannot look at a buzzard on the side of the road or anywhere else without this coming into my mind's eye. The State had set the stage first by moving the jury to the gravity of this heinous crime. The sheer horror of what the roadside worker saw led into evidence that would come out in the hours and days that lay ahead.

Next, Attorney Greene started a chronological diary of what took place the night my brother disappeared, and the days after. According to the testimony from a waitress at the lounge, Griffin had tried to start trouble with staff and customers. He grabbed her and made sexual advances toward her. He was warned not to, which seemed to work for the time being. He was intoxicated, but continued to be served alcohol. Further testimony by Pat's friends revealed Griffin had tried to start trouble on the dance floor; only this time Pat was his target. Pat was dancing with a friend when he accidentally bumped into the back of Griffin. Griffin then turned around and picked Pat up by his arm with what was described as a glaring and threatening look of hate toward Pat. Pat succeeded in apologizing and trying to diffuse the situation , then the dancing resumed. Pat later ran into Griffin again in the restroom, where Griffin asked him for a ride home. Pat readily obliged, hoping to restore the peace further. Pat, telling his friends he would be right back, left with Griffin in his car. It just so happened that a Deputy Sheriff was driving through the parking lot of the lounge and asked Pat where he was going with Douglas Griffin, as he was aware of the violent-natured man Griffin was, and knew Pat was the opposite. The deputy testified that Pat told him he was giving Griffin a ride home, and they left. This was the last time Patrick Dale was seen alive.

The testimony then led to a friend of Griffin's that lived in Tuscaloosa. She testified he called her from a lounge in Tuscaloosa on Saturday, July 16, and she went to meet him there. He had a different car along with a significant amount of cash on hand. The two of them, according to her, partied and drank for several days and nights at her house. She saw a shotgun in the car, along with the personal effects of another person. Later, Patrick's wallet was recovered there containing his driver's license and a picture of my parents. No money was in the wallet. There were bloodstains in the front seat of the car. She did not say or do anything about this, even though she was suspicious, but knowing Griffin as long as she had, was afraid of what he might do if she questioned him. After their time together, he sold the car to her son-in-law for $200, and took a bus back to Evergreen. He left the shotgun with a relative and told him not to tell anyone about it. She testified that she knew Griffin had done something terribly wrong, she but did not do or say anything further at that time. After he got back to Evergreen, he drank a bottle of whiskey and took a month's worth of pills he was prescribed by Bryce Hospital in Tuscaloosa. His parents took him to the Evergreen Hospital with a diagnosis of overdose and attempted suicide. His mother had asked him where the gun went, and he told her, "I killed a boy."

His parents were in the courtroom, and I had empathy for what they were going through. At the same time, I looked at my parents, and saw and felt the raw emotions they, my siblings, and I were sharing: emptiness, anger, despair, intense sadness, and the excruciating pain Pat had endured. I asked myself, "If someone is a confirmed violent mental patient, why in the world would one allow a gun within arm's reach of that person?" It was established at this time in the trial that early in the morning of July 16, 1983, Pat had driven Griffin to his home about five miles from the lounge. Griffin told Pat he was going inside to get $5 for gas, only to walk out a minute later in the darkness with a shotgun down by his side. He got into the passenger side, pointed the gun at Pat, and forced him to drive north into the night.

The testimony shifted to Griffin's violent past, with multiple indictments for violent behavior, but none of them were ever carried out. It was brought out that he was a "trouble maker" in the mental hospital, and was discharged because he was uncooperative with the therapy. It was also revealed that he had easy access to the gun that he held on the paraplegic farmer and used to killed Pat: A sawed-off, double-ought shotgun.

There were pictures of Pat's car where it was discovered in the parking lot of the hospital. It had been abandoned there by the son-in-law, as he was becoming aware of what was happening in the days following his purchase of the stolen car. Amanda's struggle with the car being at her place of employment made her already fragile condition worse, as she was pregnant with her second child. We, as a family, convinced her that seeing his car would have changed nothing, and the murder happened long before Tuscaloosa came into the picture. The car, a beautiful white 1975 Chrysler Cordoba, was one of Pat's prides, as he loved his vehicles and took immaculate care of every one he ever owned. It was worth way more than the $200 that Griffin illegally sold it for. Pat was an excellent auto mechanic. My father instilled in all of us that if we took care of our cars, they would serve us well for many years. It was with the Wilcox County Law Enforcement as key evidence for the case.

Witness after witness took the stand revealing a trail of drinking and spending money that Griffin previously did not have. The days following were some of the most difficult days of my life. This was when we learned what really happened after Pat left the lounge. I had been haunted about the pain that Pat might have endured after being kidnapped. What does one feel when they realize they might die in moments? The sheer panic and fear; the bargaining he must have attempted under such circumstances, with a madman holding a shotgun to his head while he drove into the darkness. The hope he tried to hold onto with every plea to Griffin not to kill him. Then, ultimately realizing he was to die anyway, not being able to say goodbye to his family, the little girl he loved so much, and others he was so devoted to. This must be the most pain any human could endure; the pain and horror of the crime and knowing your life is about to end, and there is nothing further that could be done to prevent it.

Investigator Chuck Gibson took the stand. He was chief investigator for the State. His testimony was laden with hard evidence and details that led to an undeniable conclusion of Griffin's guilt. It painted the picture of a calculated plot for Griffin to get to Tuscaloosa with a car and money, with absolutely no regard for anyone else but himself. The crime scene revealed why it was no surprise that the first witness, the man who initially discovered Pat's remains, was so shaken that day of discovery. Investigator Gibson, along with Attorney Greene exposed the jury to every detail of that crime scene.

Mr. Gibson began telling the jury about the scene as he found it. He said that Patrick's badly decomposed body was initially found in an area in Wilcox County, between the towns of Camden and Selma, which is about forty miles north of Evergreen. The body had been intentionally covered with sticks and brush. As the first witness stated at the beginning of the trial, buzzards flew away as he approached it. It was apparent that the body had been decapitated at the time of the murder. The evidence showed that Patrick Dale and Douglas Griffin, heading north, had pulled off at a remote roadside area on the right side of the road that had only a picnic table. It was assumed and agreed that Griffin had ordered Pat to pull off so he could urinate. Evidence showed blood was in the front seat of the car and on the outside of the driver door, indicating that Pat had been hit in the head with the butt of the shotgun while inside the car. Griffin removed the key from the ignition and got out on the passenger side with gun in hand. Then Pat got out of the driver side, most likely attempting to flee the area. Griffin then shot Pat at point blank range, and Pat went down. According to the forensic report, the blast tore apart his chest cavity. Evidence showed that Griffin walked up to Pat on the ground, and pointing the gun upward under his chin, shot Pat again in the head, nearly decapitating him. Griffin's limited intelligence led investigators to reason he did this so Pat could not be identified. Griffin then dragged Pat's dead and mangled body by his legs across the road about eighty feet into a wooded area and placed sticks and brush over his remains. The location where Pat was shot contained shattered teeth, bone fragments, and Pat's eye glasses. It showed the initial shot was to his torso at very close range, probably less than ten feet.

This was where he emptied Pat's pockets, taking his money and wallet. There was change lying on the ground, his jean pockets were inside out, and his right arm was missing. It was assumed it had been torn off by an animal of some sort.

Uncle John later told me he and Aunt Pearl went to the crime scene days later, and some of Pat's hair was still on the ground at the area where his body had lain for so many days. There was a silhouette left behind where the blood and fluids had left his body. It occurred to me to wonder why the crime scene people would leave his hair behind, which was the only thing left of his head. This was part of his remains, and should have gone with the rest of him. The State attorneys had several color photos of Pat's body and the entire crime scene. They tried at least half a dozen times to enter the pictures of Pat's remains into evidence to the jury, but the Defense fought that to the end. The judge never allowed the pictures to be shown. The reasoning was at least five days had passed from the actual murder, and the body had been subject to high temperatures, sun, vultures, and other animals, all of which had taken their toll on the remains, therefore grossly deteriorating the true condition of the body at the time of death. The pictures were extremely graphic in nature. I never wanted to view them; that was not Pat, my living brother, but his remains after a brutal attack and mutilation. Some members of my family wanted to view the pictures, but I talked them out of it as Pat would not have wanted us to see him in that way. I do understand why the State tried so vehemently to have these pictures entered as evidence – to move the jury's emotions. The main objective was to get a capital murder conviction and ultimately a death sentence. When this day in court neared the end, the horror Pat endured that night came to light.

The dark place we were taken when this segment ended was so unbearable for me and my family. My parents were sitting in front of me when this all came out. None of us could hold back the groans and sobs. I seemed to be at the crime scene on that night. I was feeling Pat's horror and pain. I witnessed and felt the unspeakable pain my father was in at that time. Attorney Greene's voice was cracking with emotion as he had to describe this, as well as Investigator Gibson. The courtroom was so moved by the compelling story, the judge called for a recess.

My cousins were trying to console us. At the time of recess, Judge Norton said, "Get him out of here!" referring to Griffin, wanting him out of his presence and courtroom. We had to walk right by Griffin to exit the courtroom. Looking straight toward him, I know the contempt and disdain I was feeling was obvious. I even turned toward him as I walked by, tempted to jump the half-fence and strangle him, but I went on out of the room. The next day he was surrounded by extra protection, having two more officers around him.

The Defense:

Douglas Griffin entered a plea of self-defense. His version of the story was weak, and the evidence did not support it. He stated that he and Pat had decided to drive north to see some girls that Pat knew. He claimed they were going to pawn the shotgun and that's why he went inside and got it. He stated they put the gun in the trunk and, after driving for about an hour, Pat pulled off the side of the rode to urinate. He went to the trunk, pulled out the gun and pointed it at Griffin to rob him, telling him he was going to leave him there. A struggle ensued, and Griffin grabbed the gun back and accidentally shot Pat, killing him. This held no water, of course, and was not consistent with the evidence of the crime scene. It did not correspond to the evidence that Pat was shot at approximately a ten-foot range, the width of the car, then shot a second time to conceal his identity, dragged into the brush, his pockets emptied, and then Griffin partying for days following the crime. Prosecutors reiterated the difference in stature of the two men, the violent nature of Griffin, and his multiple past indictments. It was a no-brainer. Griffin's defense was so weak, I heard one of the defense attorneys say he was "so guilty" and there was nothing more they could do than try to prevent the death penalty. They did this by using information from his past, of him having a low IQ along with mental problems, then they started leaning toward the insanity plea. This did not go far, due to the confrontation with the staff at the Holiday Inn lounge, his violent past, and the events following the murder that night. He clearly had a plan when he first abducted Pat, and he followed it through.

The next day, closing statements by the State were intended to move the jury toward the death penalty. It was intentionally graphic in nature, and pointed to a killer that forfeited his right to life by taking an innocent life in such a hateful and violent manner. In order to have capital murder stand as a charge, there must be a forced kidnapping, premeditated murder, and a robbery, all of which were proven. The Defense's closing statements were that of empathy for Griffin, and emphasis toward the jury that if they recommended the death penalty, they too would be guilty of killing another person. The trial lasted five days. The jury deliberated only twenty-eight minutes. The verdict was guilty of capital murder. He was off to Holman State Prison. The trial started on a Monday morning and ended on a Friday afternoon.

Griffin was escorted in handcuffs out of the courtroom and down an elevator. The Montgomery Advertiser reporter Alvin Benn, who had been closely following and reporting the trial every day, went down the stairwell to capture a picture of Griffin being escorted out of the courthouse. Outside, he got close to Griffin for the picture, and was standing next to the same Deputy who saw Patrick in the parking lot of the Holiday Inn that fateful night. Griffin, in his usual evil mentality, tried to kick Benn, but instead kicked the Deputy.

We left the Wilcox County Courthouse, relieved that it was over but emotionally drained. It was like living Pat's death over again. It was a different but equal pain as we finally learned what really went down that night in the woods and in the days that followed. A short time later, the jury recommended life without parole. The sentence was handed down by the judge several weeks after the trial. He followed the jury's recommendation of life without parole. This was not accepted well at all by certain members of my family, especially my parents and sister. The verdict later left us empty and unsatisfied that Griffin did not get the death penalty.

My parents have to drive by the house that Griffin lived in every time they visit Pat's grave. The pain will never end, and one man still lives. An innocent man's life was brutally wiped off the face of the earth forever. A family lost a son, brother, and father. Some things we know we cannot change, but other things we can. Some things we can fight to change, and we must. The battle was not over for my father.

Chapter 5

After the Murder Trial

Christmas came just after the trial. It was every bit as dark as the one the year before. The huge, gaping hole at family gatherings was painfully evident; the empty chair at Christmas dinner. My father's heart was broken, and we all worried about his health. He still had his business, but he was leaning on making changes and possibly leaving town. The months following the murder trial brought forth new avenues and challenges in pursuing justice. It was evident to me that several laws had been broken or, to say the least, there was questionable conduct in the dealings and happenings of Griffin. Why was he discharged from Bryce Hospital when he was still homicidal? Why were so many indictments brought against him in his past but never carried through? Why was he still served alcohol at the Holiday Inn Lounge after being deemed intoxicated? These were questions that needed answers and my father was in pursuit of them.

In the meantime, Griffin appealed the ruling and fought to reverse his conviction, which failed miserably. The Court of Criminal Appeals of Alabama attempted to overturn Griffin's conviction in 1986. The argument was that Griffin claimed he was not given his

Miranda Rights within the correct standard of law; he had taken Ludiomil the day of the murder and mixed it with alcohol, therefore impairing his judgment; and he was coerced into a confession. None of this stood up in the murder trial of 1984; all of the allegations by Griffin were easily disputed. He remains to this day in the maximum security prison in Alabama with his conviction of life without parole.

On January 28, 1985

Emmett Dale, father and administrator of his deceased son Patrick Dale, proceeded to file a law suit on nine charges of the Wrongful Death of his son. Charges were brought against the following: Douglas Griffin for the murder of Patrick Dale; The Alabama Department of Mental Health, Bryce Hospital, Northwest Alabama Mental Health Center including the psychiatrists, medical doctor, and other certain staff that evaluated, treated, and discharged Douglas Griffin back into society while in a homicidal state; Holiday Inn Eufaula, Holiday Inn Inc., which owned the Holiday Inn Evergreen, which was an A.B.C. Board licensee (Alcohol Beverage Control) of the lounge in the Holiday Inn in Evergreen, for serving Griffin after being deemed visibly intoxicated; and CIBA pharmaceuticals that manufactured Ludiomil, the medication that Griffin was taking at the time of Patrick's death. Trial Attorneys Jere Beasley and Greg Allen took on the case. Combined charges demanded judgment of $25,000,000.00 and cost of action.

Griffin's Past; Leading Up to the Murder

In researching the violent and troubled past of Douglas Griffin, one must ponder how he was allowed to wander through society a free man. His violent behavior, mental illness, and drug and alcohol abuse was clearly documented throughout his young adult life. His long history of arrests and violence started in 1977, as a young man. These included multiple DUIs, domestic and severe physical violence against his wife, stealing from his grandmother, writing bad checks, pointing a gun on an employer and threatening to kill him, fraud, and on and on. It is documented he discussed his violence and previous arrests with the intake staff at a hospital after being involuntarily admitted. He had been a patient at multiple drug and alcohol rehab facilities throughout the state, and been in jail many times also. Interviews are documented that "he had suicidal and homicidal ideations and attempts in the past, as well as hallucinations and auditory delusions." He enlisted in the Alabama Army National Guard in October 1982, and was called to active duty in January of 1983. Within one month of active duty he was discharged from the National Guard because he was deemed to have severe mental illness by his counselors and commander. In early 1983, Griffin attempted to enter an Alcoholism Recovery Center in Birmingham, but was denied admission indicating that Griffin was "obsessed with suicide and murder." Later on April 8, 1983, he was committed to Bryce Hospital in Tuscaloosa. There he was transferred to the substance abuse unit on April 14. A clinical psychologist, medical doctor, and a unit coordinator were in charge of the treatment and decision-making regarding Griffin's treatment. An IQ test was performed, and he was deemed to have an IQ of about eighty. He was given a battery of psychological tests; however, he was uncooperative and refused to complete them. What results they did complete revealed that he displayed "sociopathic and paranoid personality traits" and alcoholism was secondary to his "personality deficits." Even with this information, he remained in the substance abuse unit and no further psychological testing or treatment was ever carried out. His estimated date of release from Bryce Hospital was set for June 1, 1983, after he was to have completed a course of substance abuse and psychological treatment, which never happened. In late April, he had written a letter to his wife stating that he was going to escape ("sneak out") the hospital and kill himself, and possibly her, but first he was "going to kill a lot of other people". She notified the Northwest Alabama Mental Health Center, which in turn notified the staff of Bryce Hospital. Despite the letter of intent to kill, he was released into society on May 4, 1983, almost one month before his scheduled release date. The doctors at the Alabama Board of Mental Health obtained the letter. They had it in their possession, and submitted it to his doctors in Bryce. Even so, it was documented by the medical doctor that Griffin was discharged "because he was wasting space and not cooperating with the program." Upon his discharge from Bryce Hospital, Griffin went to Chicago. In Maywood, he was sent back to Alabama, per Griffin's testimony at the trial, by the police. He stated that the police of Maywood "made sure I was put on a bus going back to Alabama."

In early July, the supervising attorney for Bryce Legal Aide who was representing Griffin in his divorce, formally requested to withdraw from the case to represent Griffin as "he was not competent to assist her, he could not make rational decisions, couldn't understand her, and no attorney client relationship could be maintained due to his mental condition." It was around that time that he held a shotgun on a paraplegic farmer near Evergreen and threatened to kill him, but the farmer talked him out of it. The farmer dropped charges because he was afraid of Griffin. Two weeks later, he gunned down my brother Patrick Dale in the early morning hours of July 16, 1983, with that same double-ought shotgun that was easily accessible at his parents' home where he was residing at that time.

His severe mental illness was clearly apparent and documented within the state mental health system of Alabama, but he remained a free man in society.

Outcomes of the Lawsuit:

The case of the makers of the drug Ludiomil was dismissed. The Holiday Inn charge was clear and concise, as there was substantial evidence of the intoxicated state of Griffin upon his arrival at the lounge. The companion that was with Griffin before their arrival testified in court that they had been drinking most of the afternoon. He stated "Griffin had consumed approximately a third of a gallon of beer as well as four to five cans." The lounge did not follow the A.B.C. laws set forth in operating a drinking establishment. According to testimony, Griffin continued to be served alcohol after being deemed intoxicated, so they settled, and the Holiday Inn in Evergreen subsequently closed. As a result of the $200,000 dollar settlement, Holiday Inn Inc. and Holiday Inn Eufala were released from the suit.

The State of Alabama Department of Mental Health, Bryce Hospital, and the three defendants that managed Griffin's case, as previously described, were found liable for wrongful death in civil court. The defense of immunity due to being state employees and a state institution was overturned due to negligence. These parties subsequently appealed in the Court of Civil Appeals on grounds of sovereign immunity. It was obvious that the parties involved with the care and treatment of Griffin during his time in Bryce Hospital and after his release into society were clearly negligent, with documentation to back it up. He was a danger to the public at the time of his release as previously described in detail. Even when the state attorney, who was employed by the hospital, released him as a client (divorce case) due to mental illness, he was still allowed to roam society, knowing full well he had intentions of homicide and suicide. My father and trial lawyer Greg Allen and his firm fought the state of Alabama all the way to the State Supreme Court, only to have the judgment for wrongful death of Patrick Dale reversed due to the fact that Bryce Mental Hospital was a state-run institution; the doctor, psychiatrist, and staff were state employees; and the Department of Mental Health was state-run as well. The final judgment by the Alabama State Supreme Court held that "the defendants are entitled to the umbrella of substantive, or qualified, immunity from civil liability." This was after more than a three-year fight with Emmett Dale and attorney Greg Allen and his firm prevailing up until this moment, June 1988.

This very case to this day has made it almost completely impossible in Alabama for any state institution, or employee, to be held liable for wrongful death. Additionally, it has upheld exclusive immunity from almost any lawsuit, no matter what action or lack thereof has or has not been done. How does this protect society and the general public as a whole? It does not; as a matter of fact, it does the opposite of protecting society.

Chapter 6

Three Huge Obstacles to Overcome

1.) Exclusive Immunity of State from liability of a wrongdoing, wrongful death, or negligence.

This case proved beyond a shadow of a doubt that Griffin was not stable at the time of his discharge, and the actions he carried out following discharge led to the death of Patrick Dale. Even with this being established, the staff and Alabama Department of Mental Health were not held liable at the level of the State Supreme Court due to a technicality of the law. The defendants were found guilty of the wrongful death of Patrick Dale. Pat would not have died that night if the state had performed its duties and not discharged Griffin into society, knowing full well he was homicidal and a danger to the public. Remember, he was discharged due to being "uncooperative and taking up space." He never had a complete psychological evaluation and certainly did not complete his psychological treatment. He was discharged almost a full month ahead of his scheduled date. In the eyes of law, it was established that Griffin was not the only guilty party here. In order for society and the public at large to live without fear of being randomly murdered, this technicality in the law must be re-examined and reversed.

This Immunity law originated by virtue of the 11th Amendment, ratified in 1795, which granted sovereign immunity to states. This was the result of an individual from one state suing another state for payment on goods supplied to the other state during the Revolutionary War. It was never meant to apply to wrongful death cases. Since then, it has been interpreted in at least four different ways. The big question is whether a state has full sovereignty, complete independence from law, or partial sovereignty. There has been case upon case of sovereign immunity upheld and not upheld, extending all the way to the Federal Supreme Court. The law has been used, twisted, and exploited to allow anyone or any institution, whether a hospital, university, office of law enforcement, etc., that is state- run to have exclusive immunity even when the crime committed has been proven by a court of law. In other words, a law or laws have been broken, but immunity prevails no matter what. Everything that was established and found to be true in the courts can be erased and deemed nonexistent.

It is peculiar to me, in researching the cases I have and this one in particular, that the Defendants can never claim in their defense that they did not commit the crime. Each time they just claim immunity. They cannot deny the fact(s) that what they did or did not do was unlawful. They just claim immunity, every time. It is high time this used and abused law of sovereignty be modified to protect the citizens of this country. Until this is accomplished, innocents will continue to die due to the action or inaction of negligent institutions and people.

2.) With gun ownership comes much responsibility.

Responsible gun ownership; this must be addressed by our nation as a whole. The 2nd Amendment is the law of the land. That is not up for debate. Responsible gun ownership is what is up for debate. Not everyone should be able to own a firearm, nor should they have access to one.

Anyone that owns a firearm must keep it locked up and inaccessible to a child. This is a law that is in effect in some states, but is not enforced. Many gun owners have a lackadaisical attitude about this. Three children die every day due to accidental shootings in this country. The National Rifle Association is actively opposed to safe gun storage laws. Why? This safe gun storage should also apply to anyone who has been involuntarily committed to a mental hospital and diagnosed with severe mental illness, has been incarcerated due to violent behavior with a firearm, or deemed unsafe to be around a firearm in the court of law, just as convicted felons cannot own guns. Recall that Douglas Griffin took the gun in the house he was living in; his parents' house. The shotgun actually belonged to his father. It should have been locked up and out of Griffin's reach.

Universal background checks with all gun sales should be mandated across the country with a federal database, the NCIS (National Instant Criminal Background Check System). This has been a monumental issue that seems to be stuck in quicksand. It seems that both sides of the aisle agree that background checks should be performed on anyone purchasing a firearm, but nothing is being implemented to get a system in place. Research indicates that very few states are reporting severely mentally ill people to the database, and mental institutions that are reporting this are almost nonexistent. HIPAA laws protect them in many instances, and certain gun rights advocates are using this as a shield. How about protecting the general public from a psychotic and homicidal gun owner? Also, some states only use paper in their reporting, which by today's standards is primitive to say the least. There is no excuse for this. This cannot be blamed on any single entity, but all parties that are involved in the sale and control of guns should take the common sense approach: Guns should not be accessible to children or severely mentally ill and violent people. Please note this does not apply to all mentally ill people, but specifically severely and dangerous mentally ill people. The argument is not about the 2nd Amendment, it is about common sense and responsible gun ownership. It's as simple as that. There is a middle ground. And for the sake of humanity, we as a nation must achieve this. This is not a political issue, this is a human issue.

3.) There is no Baker Act Law in Alabama, nor most other states.

The Baker Act Law exists in Florida. It states that if a person is a danger to him/herself or others, or mentally ill to the point of danger to himself or others, he or she can be involuntarily committed for evaluation by a licensed psychiatrist for up to 72 hours. This action can be taken by a medical professional, law officer, or a judge. In Alabama, many times involuntary admission to a mental facility can be time-consuming and extremely difficult. This difficulty may ultimately allow the person to carry out his or her intent to do harm or kill, simply because getting them committed was troublesome. This is another issue that must be dealt with at the national level to keep the public safe. There is a monumental problem with what is happening among much of the mentally ill population in this country.

There are not enough people paying attention to this matter; they are only sweeping this deadly issue under the bureaucratic rug. This is willful ignorance, and it will ensure innocent people keep dying every day.

4.) This was a murder trial between the State of Alabama (Patrick Dale) and Douglas Griffin.

The State won and Griffin was sentenced to life without parole, and is still in Holman State Prison. The State fought for Patrick. Then the State fought all the way to the State Supreme Court, against Patrick, the same victim it previously fought for. It blames Griffin and yes, he was guilty, but others were guilty also. It was proven in court. From the standpoint of a layperson such as myself where law is not my area of expertise, this is somewhat of an oxymoron. The latter case appears to be not what is right or wrong in the eyes of the justice system, but what can the justice system do to protect state employees when they break the law, no matter what happened or who died. Again, this boils down to just plain common sense. This case does not make sense. This must be dealt with and modified to protect society. One would assume that when the malpractice suit was brought forth, the justice system transferred the case of Patrick Dale's gruesome and horrific murder to someone else within the Justice system in Montgomery. Without another thought, they handed it over, put on their hat, and went home to their family, sleeping well at night and thinking that all was well with the world.

Afterword

My family hasn't been the same since that fateful night of July 16, 1983. The vision of what Pat endured while driving his car for miles into the night begging for his life as a crazy man sat next to him, aiming a shotgun to his head, is a constant dark and painful memory forever implanted in our hearts and souls. What went down on the side of that road will haunt every one of us for the rest of our lives. The mere glimpse of a vulture on the side of a road eating a carcass takes me back to my brother's blown up and rotting body laying for five days in the hot summer sun, only to be ravaged and eaten. Seeing what my father endured in the days and years following Pat's death is almost more than one can imagine.

A little girl lost the only father she ever knew. A father was never able to groom his son to take over his business. A family was never able to celebrate Christmas or another birthday with Pat. A young man was never able to realize his full potential and leave a positive mark in this world, nor was he ever able to laugh, cry, dance, or fall in love again.

The worst happened to Patrick Dale that night, but it did not have to happen. Crimes like this will continue to happen as long as the "Justice System" does not practice what, by mere definition, it is supposed to practice: Justice.

Until the people of this country see and feel the pain of so many others, nothing will change to protect those we love. Take off your blinders. This is not a political issue. This is a human issue and it must not be ignored any longer. Thirty years ago, Douglas Griffin was discharged from a mental hospital and had access to a sawed off shotgun. Thirty years later, it is still just as likely to happen. We as a country, and many new lawmakers, are regressing to a "Cowboy Mentality," disavowing any self-responsibility for dangerous, mentally ill people or responsible gun ownership. Does society think it is immune from becoming a victim of these senseless killings? Well, you are not. Pat was an easy target, because he was a decent and caring person.

We must act now. If we live in a so-called "civilized" society, then we as a collective must act "civil." Change must come, the time is nigh. If we don't act now, we will regress back to the primal, archaic society we evolved from. The pain will only continue. From the public at large, the medical community, government-run agencies, the justice system, to our top government officials and lawmakers, we must take accountability and be responsible for our actions in order to maintain a free, safe, and civilized society.

My father, Emmett Dale, passed away at the age of eighty-seven while I was writing this book. I never told him what I was doing because it would have taken him back into the darkness and pain that he carried with him for the last thirty years. He was at peace when he died. I know now they are together again. I do not want his pain or Pat's premature death to go one more day in vain. I dedicate this to all of the victims of these senseless acts of gun violence, and Patrick and Emmett Dale, my beloved brother and father.

 Betsy Dale Adams grew up in the seventies surrounded by a close family in the small town of Evergreen, Alabama. She had a propensity to help people, which may be the reason she became a registered nurse. Betsy always enjoyed writing, though she carried this story in her heart and soul for over thirty years without writing a word about it. She knew one day it would find its way onto paper. After the thirtieth anniversary of her brother's death, it was time to sit down and let it out. Realizing the importance of this story with its relevance to social problems that exist in our country today, she hopes readers will understand and help make necessary changes that may save lives in the future. Betsy resides in Northwest Florida with her husband, Pat.